For Joe

Acknowledgements

Train Journey to Melbourne and *The Frangipani Tree* first appeared in Sarasvati magazine.

Thanks are due to Elizabeth Burns who has gently mentored my poetry for several years, and Mollie Baxter who has provided cups of tea and sound advice on my writing. Hugs are due to my husband, Chris who has listened to my poems, proof read them and helped me create a good order for this book. Last but by no means least I want to thank all at IDP for publishing my early poems and giving me the confidence to work at my writing. Dawn, you are a joy to work with, your comments mean so much.

The Memory Tree is Angela Christopher's first collection.

CONTENTS

The Memory Tree

The Reunion

In Cordoba's old town, we sit in a tiled café,
watching Spanish families meet and greet each other,
with kisses on both cheeks and lots of wild embracing.
I'm inviting my absent family to lunch in a private room.
At a table with red napkins I order tapas, wine, water.
Grandma walks in, hairpins falling from her bun,
my mother in her worn mac and sensible shoes.
Father takes off his old tweed cap and smiles,
'Nice little place you've found, I'll pay.'
Aunty rushes in, all rosy cheeks, hair like spun hay.
I watch the door, see raindrops clinging to his hair,
hands full of books. His rucksack pushes past a waiter.
My son looks young, we raise and clink glasses,
chatter wraps around me like a long-missed hug.
A little drunk, I blow kisses to special people,
until noise drifts away, the table shrinks,
and loneliness grips me with cold, bony hands.

Near Alicante

Walking to the beach past pines and sandy dunes,
silver tree-trunks dappled with shadows,
we find silky, purple daisies with ragged petals
in a glade, near yellow pompom flowers.
The sea is turquoise clear and cold.
A girl splashes water, dancing in the nude,
white breasts moving to their own tune.

On the beach, arches of bleached branches,
we listen to the whoosh and clash of waves.
You tell me you're having a bad day, have nothing to say.
In the pine forest I gaze at the sky, wind plays with my hair.
I feel the ghost of a bleak future, I give my pain to the trees.
Asleep early, you're safe from the illness you hate.
I'm alone in the middle of Spain, writing to keep my sanity.

History

Outside Cordoba's mosque are cypress trees,
a pool of water shines with coins tossed in as a prayer.
Inside, murmuring dim spaces, oil lamps like wide dishes,
candy-striped arches. Tides of people stare
at the cathedral inside the mosque. In cool tiled pathways
are high domed ceilings, gold patterned arches.
Stimulated by history, you come alive,
talk on the Roman bridge about Islamic culture,
as the green Guadalquivir River slopes past.
Walking in the Jewish quarter, we hear echoes of men
studying philosophy, maths, poetry. Nine hundred years
ago on these stones, feet scurried to the synagogue.
We feel the light touch of drifting ghosts.

Winter in Australia

Orange rocks loom over Redhead beach,
under a blue sky. Giant breakers tumble,
roll, rumble, crashing in flying mists of spray,
foam bubbles slide and slip down sand.

Shoe and paw prints trail in lines along the shore,
shadows give me long legs walking in surf
under a sinking sun, the ocean sucks and crashes.
Empty coal ships wait to take black cargoes

to pollute the air in China, where masked
Chinese struggle to breathe poisoned smog.
Driving home, amber light washes over the forest,
turning bamboo into flaming, feathery gold.

Queenstown

We fly over peaks like carved clouds,
glacier lakes glitter, veins of ice trickle
down steep rock sides.

Outside the Air New Zealand plane,
blue skies, white snow, clean air.
A sign says, 'Thank you for helping us

protect our way of life.' In the airport
they examine shoes, boots, for traces
of foreign earth. Later in a room

over Lake Wakatipu, evening sun
flushes mountains, rock crevices
deepen with shadows, snow peaks

look cut out against a rising moon,
and the lights of Queenstown
rise up the hill like stars.

Coronet Peak

Glassy ski runs seem to touch the sky,
stick people dance as they swoop
down, powdered snow whips spray
like smoke behind them. Ice scribbles
made by skis shine like snail trails.
Halfway down the slopes, colours
seep into jackets, the swoosh
and scrape of snowboards gets louder,
figures fly down steep white cliffs.
Screwing up my eyes I see sunspots
and a blinding white universe.
Lottie shuffles onto a moving carpet,
taking her up to the nursery slope.
She slides between her mother's legs,
then she's on her own, hands on knees.
A three-year old in red boots gliding free.

Playing with Barney

'All the animals are in the dark wood,'
he said, crawling into his mother's closet.
'Can you see an eye?'
'What is it?' I said.
'It's a tiger, sssh,' he said,
pointing to a heap of black clothes.
'Oh no, the tiger's waking up, let's run,' he said.
We crawled behind the sofa, squashed
by a line of orange balloons.
'What are these?' I said.
'Very, very big mountains,
see the kangaroo does big jumps.'
'And the dingo?'
'He runs fast.'
'And the lizard?'
'He crawls like this.'
'What about koala?'
'He'll have to stay here till morning.'
'Please save her,' I said, 'she's scared.'
'All right, kangaroo will carry her.'
'Are they safe now?' I said.
'No, you be silly, there's the river, they all cross together,'
he said, clutching the animals across the cushion river.
'Then they go back to their rock,' I said.
'It's morning now, they all wake up.'
'Barney, it's bedtime.'
'One more story when they fight the tiger.'
'Think about that in bed,' I said.

Train Journey to Melbourne

I'm pulling apart from grandchildren,
a stretched out silence, away from their voices.
We see bleached gum-trees, seas of straw scrubland,
farm machinery on verandas near the track,
corn stacked in fields, hear the clack of train wheels.

I'm lying on bean bags looking out at bamboo,
listening to shouts from the trampoline, 'Nana, look at me.'
Pulling a bath of water along the hot deck,
baby Lottie giggles, splashes, throwing up fat hands.

Through the train windows are sluggish brown rivers,
stranded trees lying across muddy water.
Near Campbelltown, black cattle crowd under branches,
at Cootamundra, white leafless trees against an azure sky.

Platinum pathways wind through forests,
bungalows' aluminium roofs shine near grey hills.
On Wagga Wagga station a young man kisses his crying lover.
At Wangaratta the dusty run down North Eastern Hotel.

I see the circus again, watch the girl
doing splits, handstands in mid-air,
while a posse of youngsters stand, mouths open.
By the lake at sunset the baby throws stones in the water,
her brother dances with glow sticks. 'Nana look at me.'

Staring out at sheep trapped in shade,
I sense all close connection has snapped.

Sky Deck Melbourne

We climb to the eighty-eighth floor,
watch globules of cars swim in black skyscrapers,
giant glass buildings ripple with reflections.
Matchstick canoes collect on the brown river;
sun pixelates water into shivering diamonds;
stick-people walk on bridges, stepping on shadows.
Yellow taxis are toys; strings of moving cars
silver streamers. It all looks slow-paced, orderly,
screened from noise. The real city, with rumbling trams
and screeching tyres, gone, replaced by neat grid
roads, straight lines, silence. Even the roof gardens
don't look real, with lollipop bushes and tiny people
lying like pegs on invisible sun loungers.

By night, colours explode,
fluorescent paint spattered under a black sky;
cars like moving earthbound stars
crawl along orange and blue spider's webs;
a stadium glows ghostly green, train platforms
look like fat gold bars, streets amber necklaces:
through it all the black river Yarra flows like liquorice,
as the city shows its vibrant night attire, dashes, splashes,
dots of neon, a firework festival of light.

The Jacket

A coat in British Home Stores
jerks me back to my teenage years,
to my young self, hormones swirling,
wearing this jacket over bleached jeans.

In a picture in the sixties,
I sit on a rug, with wild hair and freckles.
My jacket smells of gorse and smoke,
my pocket hides tobacco and secret roll-ups.

I look at the camera with green eyes,
knowing I have talents my family can't see,
already a black sheep at fifteen,
living an unseen life away from home.

In art school I learn who I am, weld metal,
weave wool dyed with bark and lichen,
draw raw charcoal pictures, mould plaster,
looking like a workman in denim dungarees.

My parents and brother bond in my absence,
cakes by the fire near slow-ticking clocks,
Sunday roasts, white tablecloths,
walks by the river putting the world to rights.

'It was marvellous when you left,' my brother says.
In the picture my mother looks away from me.
She never stepped into my creative world,
didn't want to own me in that scruffy jacket.

As a child I tried on her shoes, held beaded bags,
puffed out my chest, tried to be like her. At sixteen it's war.
I smoke in fields looking at the stars, swim naked,
have sex, get drunk, kiss boys at parties lying on the floor.

Richmond Villas

I hold this house in dreams;
pink magnolia blossom opens by my brother's window;
a rope ladder takes us high among the waxy flowers.

Terrace with striped deck chairs;
rockery where bees dropped into lavender and roses;
fir tree garden with bleached washing,
where my brother's friends spilt blood,
swearing oaths in their secret club.

Conservatory, with squeaking guinea-pigs
next to potted flowers; back-kitchen, smelling of fish,
where father cleaned shoes before church;
the Rayburn where I perched in my gymslip,
searching pans and spitting hot plates.

The dining room with blue ceiling,
where I sat with grass in my hair,
bored amongst best china when the vicar came to tea,
where we hid from the priest who fancied my mother,
giggling, mouths stuffed with handkerchiefs.
The back lane where mother walked,
hands twisted with heavy bags,
where at thirteen, listening to owls
I smelt my boyfriend's smoky coat,
kissing his cigarette breath.

Years later, I park the car, see the black habits of nuns
swing silently through the rooms. The conservatory is a chapel,
the garden unloved, with paths unswept.

The Cowrie Shell

This black spotted shell,
found by father diving, sat on a mantelshelf long ago.
Holding it now, I see that room. . .

I am riding a scooter down the Wilton carpet,
seeing crimson caves in the coal fire,
and grandma on fat cushions staring at the road.

I make tents out of blankets, my skipping rope flicks the picture
where father smiles down his tropical suit,
squinting through the African sun.

The oak table is laid for tea: egg sandwiches, pasties, cup-cakes,
cut oranges filled with jelly, a teapot with scorched cosy,
a posy of cut flowers.

On a jangly piano, uncle bangs out Broadway hits,
biting the stem of his pipe. Mother's mezzo-soprano lifts
up to my box-room bed.

At Christmas, grandma plays Ring- a- Roses,
Mother comes down the hall from a long-distance call, in tears.
We hit balloons like balls, stamp tinsel into the floor.

I skip through this room in dreams,
stop to colour a clown's hat, place dominoes in rows:
trapped memories, like sand left in this cowrie-shell.

Columbia Snowfields Glacier

The bus with jumbo tyres bumps
downhill through a pure white field.
Getting out, we step onto cracking crystals,
see tinges of blue, pink and green glacier ice.

I'm in a starched world, a stretched
out silence. As ospreys wheel
above snow fields, I see brilliant white
sheets, empty chalk-white rooms,

blank canvases waiting at home.
I'm in a white-out space.
As tourists jostle and slide over slush,
I catch this wild place breathing.

Lost Lake

It lies in a semi-circle of pine trees,
glinting like crystal in the morning,
bulrushes and iris at its edge,
a backdrop of snow-capped mountains.

I swim in green water to a hot
pontoon, haul myself up a ladder,
meet girls from Washington State
who chatter and laugh like birds.

They film each other jumping into space,
catch frisbees laughing in the sun.
Chatting to them, I'm one of the young crowd
as I stretch my stiff, stubborn body.

Swimming back, fresh pond smells
remind me of Lake Garda at age fourteen:
my mother swam like a queen in her rubber hat,
before I dived off the floating deck to soak her.

By the shore, shoals of fat toad tadpoles
slither like slimy jet through my fingers .
I see you lying in the shade, curled up, eyes shut,
locked away from the magic of the day.

Whistler Mountain

Gliding to the peak, snow muffles noise,
rocks loom close, the chair lift runs
smooth as glass on steel cables,
shadows like black birds pass over the ice.

At the top a crush of snapping cameras,
a circle of white mountains.
One hairy marmot as big as a badger
climbs from his rock, scaring tourists.

Flying down, feeling close to the sky,
we see two black bears amble beneath us,
fir forests slope like steps, faraway
sweeps of green merge with turquoise lakes.

Lower down, noon heat rises to meet us,
water sprays spin under an amber sun.
We walk into a rush of bikes, sweaty riders
sweeping down summer passes.

On the mountain top,
cable cars like spiders on a web
cross the dark valley below the snow peaks.
We've returned from another world.

The Pow Wow

We sit in the Indian centre –
three Europeans among brown faces;
bass drums thud, singers' voices
rise and fall like wolves.

A woman in Indian dress
Sweeps lighted sage over faces;
hands rub scented smoke into skin,
burnt herbs smell like roast vinegar.

Women with braided hair
dance in moccasins shining with beads,
swirling silken wraps; brass bells
on dresses jingle as feet shuffle.

Other dancers hold feather fans,
feet pulse up and down to the beat.
A small boy sits on his father's knee,
banging giant drums with a stick.

Men dance alone, a boy in fringed costume
fuses Indian and street dance,
others crouch and jump like warriors,
escaped children chase around the room.

Girls copy their mothers' stepping feet;
a teenage beauty in white-beaded boots
twirls and leaps, spinning with her peacock
shawl; shining with sweat she leaves the floor.

Around the hall carvings of totem poles
show eagles, dolphins, whales; black bears
peer from cards, pendants have wolf faces,
beaded purses rainbow colours.

The frantic crescendo of drumming
feels like a fiesta. Men and women dance,
children in arms are carried onto the floor.
I thank my friend Tamara for opening this door.

The Frangipani Tree

At children's parties, only servants had black faces.
Mothers in stiff dresses drank Pimms, watching for fingers
stealing sandwiches, secretly lifting netted fly covers.
Starched children cartwheeled on the grass, caught quoits,
walked crookedly with eggs and spoons. I didn't want to race,
spied a tree with low, dark branches, slunk away from heat,
running sandals, citrus sun, walked into cool green light.
I started to climb, shaking down white waxy flowers.
King of my castle, I watched glimmers of silver serving-trays.

Then, my tree world was blown open, children's faces
pulled through leaves, they broke branches, trampled grass
to slime, lost their bow ties, slides, white socks.
This was my Kingdom, no one kept the grown-ups happy,
they stalked the grass, shielded their eyes shouting names.
The tree slowly freed its refugees, with torn shorts and dresses.
Our hostess frowned, tapped her foot, blew smoke rings in the air,
told us to behave, or she'd cancel tea. But the tree called to me.
I nibbled food, lost interest in the games, sidled back
to rock myself to sleep, in the low abandoned branches.

The Raven

In Vancouver's museum
a large sculpture* of a raven,
crouching on a giant clam.
Tiny humans cling inside the shell,
tangled heads and limbs in darkness.

A tale from the old Haida people,
from Canada's far northwest.
tells how the cunning raven
coaxed the humans out to play
onto a bright, wide beach.

All male, pale skin and black hair,
they screwed up their eyes,
terrified of this bright new world.
The trickster Raven scooped
them squeaking, under wing feathers.

Flying to the North Island,
he shook the men onto sand,
throwing moist shellfish
into their groins. The Raven laughed
as the men ran to the stormy sea.

Here, the shells dropped off,
sucking strongly onto rocks.
As rough seas of winter changed
to the soft sun of Spring, the shellfish
grew until they cracked open.

Out stepped brown skinned,
male and female humans,
not timid or weak, but strong
children of a wild coast,
making their living from the sea.

Their descendants built beach homes,
with carved totems, of eagles, bears
ravens, whales - beasts that shaped their world.
Now, villages are ruined, the sea polluted.
It's time for the Raven's return.

*The sculpture is by artist Bill Read

The Lake House

In Coniston in September, on the blue lake,
sailing skiffs line up like paper boats.
I walk into Ruskin's garden, past sweet peas
smelling of old-fashioned summer.
Under briar roses a flagstone seat, sun skims across a skein
of spider's silk. I hear distant voices, the hum of bees,
feel flies flit across my hair. Saffron light shines
through rose leaves. I wander through the house,
into the drawing room where Ruskin invited women
to dine in their prettiest dresses. A heavy photo album
shows him in his cane wheelchair looking at the sky,
woollen gloves clasped on his beard.
He wrote at dawn, looking over the lake, cat asleep by his side.
Down by the jetty, a solitary swan snaps at seaweed,
fluffing snow feathers. Waves suck and splash, stars bounce,
the horizon shimmers with quicksilver.

The Cactus Garden

They stand like totem poles
or curl their cactus limbs in a fat tangle,
growing out of black volcanic gravel:
these living sculptures dwarf people
standing majestically in a land of giants,
ribbed spines covered in a furry mass of needles.

The garden has a church-like silence:
people wander awestruck down the aisles
lined with pillars of thorny trees, handless
marrow arms defining space, showing buds
ready to spring open; large white ragged flowers
wide as grapefruits, have spindly stamens,
skeleton umbrellas. Giant hairy pincushions

burst with orange and purple daisies;
crawling cacti are full of scarlet flowers;
a prickly vase has hydrangea-like blooms;
rounded trunks with pink needles have a rosy glow.
Breezes blow, nothing moves, cacti crawl and stand,
growing slowly in stillness.

Missing You

Back from Greece, summer life scattered on the carpet,
spilled out dresses for evenings without you.
While Linda flirted with strangers, I missed holding your hand.

You met us at the airport, unshaven, with scuffed shoes,
black coat hanging off you like a flapping bird.
I still felt warm like a Greek cat stretching out on white stones.

Waking with the shock of your arms around me,
I feel my lungs rise like a helium balloon.
When I was swimming, idling away scorching days,

I thought of you, eating at this table alone,
our large house looming above you,
no lights in the sitting room, or footsteps on the stairs.

Next evening, silence seeps through doors like oil,
your grey head shines through a window.
I thought you were in bed, but you're reading the Economist,

first time in over a year; I brush away stray tears,
gulp down whisky, pray our old life is creeping back.
You frown and say, 'The Euro still faces steep risks, you know.'

Lake Geneva

After two flights we smell lemon pine,
walk into a clean, white room,
see your limp body, round dark eyes.
Your boyfriend turns his back,
to look at the silver lake.

You're lucky, a flying doctor
stopped the brain bleed.
We sleepwalk, pale with shock.
Your boyfriend's shadow closes in,
pink twilight shines in the lake.

We walk you out, you hold cardboard
coffee in pyjamas, watch swans
sail over clouds and mountain snow –
a wooden, waxy doll with listless
eyes, staring at the lake.

You fly home for heart surgery;
I hold your hand as tubes slide out.
A thin line down your chest reminds
us of that room near Lake Geneva,
looking over still blue water.

Taking your bike and clothes,
you leave that boyfriend forever,
rent a room in town, party
the nights away, singing:
'Life is for living, not for dying.'

Special Girls

I make a patchwork quilt
waiting for your arrival,
buy you summer dresses
thinking of the delivery room,
surgical sheets, transparent plastic cot.

The phone rings at five next morning:
'You have a new granddaughter –
dark hair, pretty, petite.'
Pictures beamed on e-mail show you
with baby-soft skin, lying on a hard towel,
folded pink arms like chicken wings.

On Skype, in a cobweb cardigan,
you look like a doll asleep, your dark hair pulls
me back to a London house at Christmas:
then, I held Jessica, my own baby girl,
showing her silver baubles on the tree.

I put her to bed as dusk closed in.
In my sleep I heard her father scream:
terror dripped acid through my veins.
I saw sirens, flashing lights, the last sight
of my daughter, a white-faced
limp rag-doll, carried into the night.

In the hall, Christmas cards fluttered,
tinsel shone on the floor.
Her brother and sisters stared down the road
that swallowed their baby,
looked at her empty bouncy chair.

Today in Australia, my granddaughter
sleeps in cyberspace. ‘Look at her fingers,’
says my daughter, ‘she’s got Jessica’s
special piano hands.’

Pub Night

'That band's no good,' said a man smoking in the rain.
We walked into a rush of noise, crashing drums
like waves booming onto the shore.
My ears hurt, but I tapped my feet to the beat,
as I did when you played bass at sixteen,
spotlights streaming through your hair.

This band were young lads too, rocking out songs to faint applause,
surrounded by fairy lights and men in black.
We went to the bar, crowded with skimpy girls,
stepping over sticky floors.
Thundering noise swept words from my mouth.
A young man with straggly curls put his arm around me,
his lanky body wrapped me in a hug.

When you played gigs you squeezed me, in front of your friends.
I brought you beer, stepping on the set-list sellotaped to the floor.
Before you went to University we danced around the kitchen.
You'd pick me up in a bear hug. I'd smell your curly, smoky hair.
The young man by my side bought drinks, then melted away.
'He's not your Joe, you know,' my friend said.

Listening to drums, the twanging noises and belting voices,
I sipped my wine, still missing you.

The Memory Tree

Locked inside this blue room –
no clocks, no sense of time –
just black stains on the carpet,
my body pressed inside the walls,
a depth charge sinks inside me.

Living in this blue room,
I forget to eat and wash,
my life shaken and suspended.
Outside, sparrows peck at blossom.
What does that world mean now?

Crushed inside this blue room,
I tear and cut tissue paper,
make dark pathways of branches.
Sticking yellow leaves, I see
the sunflowers at his funeral.

Wrapped inside this blue room,
I walk through an autumn maze,
each paper leaf a memory.
He is sprinkling cheese on pizza,
cleaning his bright red scooter.

Locked inside this blue room,
his rucksack has come home.
He'll never sling it in the hall again.
His memory tree grows,
surrounded by fire.

Indigo Dreams Publishing Ltd
24, Forest Houses
Cookworthy Moor
Halwill
Beaworthy
Devon
EX21 5UU
www.indigodreams.co.uk